A BUSINESS APPROACH TO RADISH FARMING

Complete Entrepreneurial Step By Step Guide To Radish Garden From Scratch

ZHURI HART

DISCLAIMER

This book is intended to provide general information and insights on adopting a business approach to farming. The content within is based on the author's knowledge and experiences up to the date of publication. It is essential to recognize that the field of agriculture is dynamic, influenced by various factors such as market conditions, climate, and regulatory changes.

Readers are advised to conduct thorough research, seek professional advice, and consider their unique circumstances before implementing any strategies or practices discussed in this book. The author and publisher disclaim any responsibility for the accuracy, completeness, or suitability of the information provided. The book is not a substitute for professional advice, and the author and publisher shall not be liable for any damages or losses arising from the use or reliance on the information presented herein.

Individual results may vary, and success in farming enterprises is contingent upon numerous variables. The author encourages readers to consult with relevant experts, agricultural extension services, and legal or financial professionals to tailor strategies to their specific needs and local conditions.

This book is not intended to be a comprehensive guide to all aspects of farming, and readers should exercise their judgment and discretion in applying the principles discussed. The author and publisher do not endorse any specific products, services, or companies mentioned in this book unless explicitly stated.

By reading this book, the reader acknowledges and accepts the inherent uncertainties in agricultural endeavors and agrees to use the information at their own risk.

TABLE OF CONTENTS

ABOUT THE BOOK

"A Business Approach to Radish Farming," a book, offers people and business owners who want to start radish farms a thorough and tactical roadmap. With a strong emphasis on the operational side of the company, the book seeks to provide readers with the knowledge and abilities needed to start and run a profitable radish farm.

The introduction establishes the framework by exploring the history of radish farming, outlining its objectives, and stressing the significance and extent of this farming endeavor. This section lays the groundwork for readers to comprehend the importance and larger context of cultivating radish in a business-oriented manner.

The book provides a thorough examination of a variety of radish farming topics. Readers acquire a comprehensive understanding of the crop by learning about the several radishes kinds, their nutritional worth, and the requirements of the land, climate, and growing seasons. Throughout the farming process, this information serves as the foundation for making wise decisions.

Important information about market trends, target client identification techniques, and the demand for radishes may be found in the market study section. Competitor analysis is included to make sure readers are ready to handle the radish market's competitive environment.

The text flows naturally into sections on crop management, quality assurance, company strategy, site preparation, and marketing tactics. A step-by-step guide to goal-setting, business plan creation, site selection, and the application of efficient crop management techniques is given in these parts.

By prioritizing quality control and adhering to industry standards, growers are able to produce radishes that satisfy both regulatory requirements and consumer expectations.

Any firm must have sound financial management, which is covered in-depth in this book through discussions of pricing strategies, budgeting, spending control, and profitability analysis. This gives readers the financial knowledge needed to manage a lucrative and sustainable radish farm.

The book also acknowledges the significance of sustainability in contemporary agriculture. It covers organic farming techniques, tackles issues of environmental effect, and places a strong emphasis on social responsibility—all of which are in line with the expanding movement toward sustainable and ethical farming approaches.

The book addresses issues that come up frequently in radish growing and offers solutions. The book makes sure that readers are equipped to handle challenges and lead their radish growing initiatives toward success by addressing potential roadblocks.

CHAPTER ONE

RADISH FARMING INTRODUCTION

THE EXTENT AND SIGNIFICANCE OF RADISH FARMING

Because radish is such a versatile root vegetable, radish farming has become more and more popular in agriculture. Beyond its culinary applications, radish farming is significant from an economic, nutritional, and environmental standpoint. Gaining an understanding of the subtleties of radish cultivation entails exploring the different varieties, nutritional value, soil and climate requirements, and growing seasons related to this lowly but important crop.

Since radish is grown all over the world, its cultivation is not limited to any one area or weather. Farmers grow radishes for a variety of purposes, from small-scale subsistence farming to commercial agriculture. Its market demand—both for fresh and processed—makes it an economically significant crop that can be used to generate revenue. Furthermore, its short growing season and low maintenance requirements add to its allure as a crop that can be grown on both a small- and large-scale.

RECOGNIZING RADISHES

Investigating the biology and traits of this cruciferous vegetable is necessary to comprehend radishes. Radishes have fleshy taproots and are members of the Brassicaceae family. Radishes are a versatile vegetable that come in a wide range of colors, shapes, and sizes to suit a variety of culinary tastes. Every variety, from the traditional red globe radish to the longer daikon, has its own distinct flavor profiles, textures, and culinary uses.

RADISHES: VARIETIES

Radishes come in a variety of varieties that highlight how adaptable this crop is to a range of tastes and growing environments. Black Spanish radishes, Watermelon,

French Breakfast, and Cherry Belle are popular varieties. Every variety has a distinct taste in addition to appearance, giving customers and foodies a wide range of options. For radish cultivation to be successful, the right variety must be chosen, taking into consideration factors like climate, soil type, and intended use.

NUTRITIONAL VALUE

The nutritious richness of radishes contributes to their attractiveness as a health-conscious choice. Radishes are low in calories and rich in vitamins, including vitamin C, fiber, and important minerals. This nutrient composition not only improves overall health but also makes radishes a beneficial supplement to balanced meals.

The eating of radishes has been connected with several health advantages, including improved digestion, enhanced immunological function, and probable antioxidant characteristics.

CLIMATE AND SOIL REQUIREMENTS

Climate and soil needs play a key influence in the effective cultivation of radishes. Radishes are noted for their adaptability to diverse temperatures, although they thrive in cool weather. Well-drained, loamy soils are good for radish growing, since they allow the roots to flourish without obstacles. Understanding the particular climatic and soil conditions required for maximum growth allows that farmers may make informed decisions regarding the timing and location of their radish crops.

GROWING SEASONS

Growing seasons for radishes vary based on the variety and area climate. While radishes are primarily cool-season crops, certain types can be produced throughout the year in suitable areas. Understanding the growth seasons is vital for planning crop rotations and maximizing the production of radishes. The ability to vary planting seasons assures a continual supply of fresh radishes, fulfilling market demands and preserving a steady crop for both farmers and customers.

There are several facets of radish farming, ranging from the financial importance of the crop to its nutritional worth and culinary adaptability. Understanding radishes entails learning about the several types, each with distinctive qualities, and appreciating how crucial soil and climate are to productive growing. Radish farming is still a dynamic and flexible agricultural technique that adds to the world's agricultural landscape despite its variable growth seasons.

CHAPTER TWO

EXAMINATION OF THE MARKET

THE NEED FOR RADISHES

A market analysis entails a thorough investigation of the several elements that impact the dynamics of supply, demand, and total availability of a specific good or service. The demand for radishes is an important factor to take into account in this situation. Businesses that operate in this industry must comprehend the elements that influence the demand for radishes. Radishes are in high demand due to consumer choices, dietary trends, and health consciousness. Furthermore, there is a growing market demand for radishes due to the growing interest in organic and locally grown vegetables.

COMMERCIAL PATTERNS

Market trends are crucial in determining the radishes landscape and businesses should keep a close eye on them. These trends cover a broad range of variables, such as shifting consumer preferences, improvements in agricultural methods, and the emergence of new agricultural technologies. For example, the market for radishes can be greatly impacted by the increasing emphasis on sustainable farming practices and the uptake of technology-driven production techniques. It is imperative for organizations to remain aware of these changes in order to adjust and take advantage of new opportunities.

DETERMINING THE TARGET MARKET

A crucial part of market analysis is identifying target customers, which helps companies to customize their tactics to the unique requirements and preferences of their target market. Regarding radishes, different characteristics including age, lifestyle, and dietary preferences may influence the target client base.

Since radishes are high in nutrients, one of the main target demographics could be health-conscious consumers. Effective marketing and product positioning strategies may be developed with the help of identifying and comprehending the traits of the target client group.

ANALYSIS OF COMPETITORS

To obtain a competitive advantage in the market, competitor analysis is essential. Analyzing competitors' advantages, disadvantages, opportunities, and dangers can give firms important information. Competitors in the radish market could be small-scale farmers or major agricultural producers. Evaluating the pricing policies, distribution methods, and marketing strategies used by rival companies can help companies figure out how to stand out from the competition and draw in customers. Businesses might also find holes in the market to exploit in order to obtain a competitive edge by analyzing the actions of their rivals.

A complete market analysis entails researching the demand for radishes, keeping an eye on industry developments, determining the target audience, and researching the competition in great detail. This comprehensive method provides organizations with the information they need to make wise decisions, create winning strategies, and negotiate the ever-changing financial market.

CHAPTER THREE

PLANNING A BUSINESS

ESTABLISHING OBJECTIVES AND GOALS

An essential first step in the company planning process is defining precise, attainable goals and objectives. Setting goals gives the organization a direction by defining the expected results and benchmarks. Conversely, objectives are time-bound, quantifiable, and specified actions that help achieve the larger aims. Setting goals and objectives entails carefully assessing the company's internal capabilities, market conditions, and mission and vision. The achievement of this strategic alignment guarantees that the objectives are both reasonable and consistent with the overarching business plan.

MAKING A BUSINESS STRATEGY

A business plan, which outlines an organization's mission, objectives, and methods for success, acts as a road map for the enterprise. The company's goal and vision, market analysis, competitive environment, marketing and sales strategies, operational goals, and financial predictions are just a few of the topics covered in this extensive document. A well-written business plan acts as a communication tool for all parties involved, including lenders, employees, and investors, in addition to giving the company a clear path. It is a dynamic document that changes as the corporate environment does, reflecting modifications to tactics and strategy.

BUDGETARY ESTIMATES

A business plan must include financial predictions since they offer an outlook on the company's financial success. The income statements, balance sheets, and cash flow statements that are included in these predictions usually forecast the period's revenues, expenses, and profitability. Robust market research, reasonable assumptions, and a profound comprehension of the market and competitive environment are prerequisites for the accuracy and dependability of financial projections. Financial forecasts are crucial for attracting investors and obtaining funding in addition to internal planning. It is imperative to periodically review and revise these forecasts in order to accommodate evolving market circumstances and company needs.

EVALUATION AND CONTROL OF RISKS

The evaluation and handling of risks are essential components of successful company planning. Recognizing possible hazards, whether internal or external, enables companies to deal with difficulties and unknowns in advance. Risks can originate from a number of different places, such as changes in regulations, market volatility, technical disruptions, and problems with internal operations.

A thorough risk management approach includes creating plans for risk reduction, setting up monitoring systems, and assessing the impact and likelihood of each identified risk. Businesses can improve their resilience and raise their chances of success by addressing risks early in the planning process. The risk management plan must be reviewed and updated on a regular basis in order to reflect changing opportunities and threats in the business environment.

CHAPTER FOUR

CHOOSING AND SETTING UP THE SITE

SELECTING THE IDEAL SITE

A crucial part of site preparation and selection is picking the ideal location, which has a direct impact on the effectiveness and success of any project. The location should be in line with the goals of the project, taking into account things like market demand, accessibility, and regulatory issues as well as closeness to resources. Making an educated choice requires examining the area's demographic profile as well as comprehending the social and economic dynamics. Long-term sustainability also requires taking possible hazards and environmental effects into account.

TESTING AND READYING THE SOIL

Testing and preparing the soil is another crucial step in the procedure. Understanding the composition, fertility, and drainage capacity of the soil is aided by carrying out comprehensive soil testing. When assessing whether the land is suitable for building or farming, this knowledge is essential. A variety of methods, including grading, leveling, and adding soil amendments to improve fertility and structure, are used in soil preparation. A solid foundation for structures is ensured by proper soil preparation, which also benefits the ecosystem's general health.

INFRASTRUCTURE NEEDS

Any development project starts with its infrastructure requirements, and the success and functionality of the project are directly impacted by how adequate they are. Evaluating the availability of energy sources, water supplies, transportation infrastructure, and telecommunications services are all part of the analysis of infrastructure needs. Sufficient infrastructure guarantees seamless operations and expedites the conveyance of products and services. In order to meet the project's needs, it is essential to assess the current infrastructure and make any necessary upgrades or enhancement plans. To solve infrastructural issues and guarantee smooth project execution, cooperation with stakeholders and local government is crucial.

Selecting and preparing a site requires a thorough strategy that includes determining the ideal location, carrying out in-depth soil testing, and attending to infrastructure needs. The successful implementation of any project, whether in the fields of building, agriculture, or other developmental initiatives, depends on the synergy between these factors. The project's sustainability and long-term success are facilitated by strategic planning, teamwork, and a deep awareness of the local environment.

CHAPTER FIVE

MANAGEMENT OF CROPS

TECHNIQUES FOR PLANTING AND CULTIVATION

Using efficient planting and cultivation methods is essential to good crop management. To guarantee the best possible crop development and output, farmers use a variety of techniques. The type of crop, the soil, and the environment all influence the planting technique selection.

Traditional techniques entail preparing the seedbed by harrowing, leveling, and plowing. Modern methods, such as no-till farming, reduce soil disturbance while preserving organic matter and enhancing water retention. With the use of cutting-edge machinery, precision planting maximizes plant spacing, minimizes waste, and allows for precise seed application. Another crucial farming technique that increases soil fertility, reduces pests, and supports sustainable agriculture is crop rotation.

SYSTEMS OF IRRIGATION

Since irrigation supplies the water required for plant growth, it is essential to crop management. Various irrigation techniques are used depending on the local conditions and crop water requirements. While conventional techniques like surface irrigation—which involves flooding fields—remain common, more effective alternatives are becoming more and more well-liked. Water is delivered to the plant's root zone directly with drip irrigation, which minimizes water waste and enhances nutrient absorption. Sprinkler systems simulate natural rainfall by distributing water over crops in a regulated manner. By combining automation and sensors, smart irrigation systems allow for precise water management, resource conservation, and agricultural production optimization.

CONTROL OF PESTS AND DISEASES

To protect plant health and guarantee a good yield, crop management must include effective pest and disease control. The comprehensive strategy known as Integrated Pest Management (IPM) blends chemical, cultural, and biological control techniques. By introducing natural predators to fight pests, biological control lessens the need for chemical pesticides. Crop rotation breaks up pest cycles and increases resistance by using resistant crop cultivars. The timely identification of pest and disease concerns is facilitated by monitoring and early detection through scouting activities. Conscious use of pesticides and encouraging beneficial insects are two examples of sustainable methods that support crop health over the long term without endangering the sustainability of the ecosystem.

PROCEDURES FOR HARVESTING

The agricultural cycle ends with harvesting, and using efficient techniques is essential to maximizing output and quality. The type, maturity, and planned use of the crop all influence when it should be harvested. Using contemporary equipment such as combine harvesters, mechanized harvesting greatly boosts productivity and lowers the need for labor. To protect crop quality and minimize losses, post-harvest processing must be done correctly. Harvested crops have a longer shelf life when stored in buildings with controlled conditions and moisture management systems. By reducing waste and maximizing resource usage, using suitable harvesting techniques guarantees a plentiful crop while also supporting sustainable agriculture.

CHAPTER SIX

STANDARDS AND QUALITY ASSURANCE

GUARANTEEING THE QUALITY OF THE PRODUCT

For companies in a variety of sectors, guaranteeing product quality is crucial. It entails using a thorough approach to uphold and enhance the standards of the products and services provided to clients. Organizations use quality control as a methodical approach to ensure that their products fulfill client expectations and certain requirements. This entails tracking and evaluating each step of the production process, from obtaining raw materials to delivering the finished product.

Strict testing procedures must be put in place in order to guarantee product quality. Both in-process testing and final product inspection may fall under this category. The ability to find flaws and departures from quality standards is greatly aided by contemporary technology like automated testing apparatus and sophisticated analytical tools. Businesses may reduce the risk of product recalls or returns, increase customer happiness, and foster brand trust by using strong quality control methods.

OBSERVING INDUSTRY GUIDELINES

Maintaining product quality and market competitiveness requires adhering to industry standards. Industry standards are set benchmarks that specify the performance requirements and acceptable quality levels for goods and services offered in a particular industry. These guidelines are frequently established by business associations, regulatory agencies, or major players by consensus. Following these guidelines promotes industry-wide uniformity, compatibility, and interoperability in addition to guaranteeing product quality.

In order to stay up to date with changing industry standards and technological breakthroughs, companies make investments in research & development. Adherence to these guidelines promotes fair trade practices and good competition in the sector, in addition to benefits for the company directly. In industries where safety, dependability, and performance are crucial, including healthcare, automotive, and electronics, meeting industry standards is extremely important.

AUTHENTICATION AND ADHERENCE:

Making sure that items adhere to legal requirements and industry standards goes hand in hand with certification. A product, procedure, or system's formal acknowledgment by a recognized authority that it conforms with particular rules or guidelines is known as certification. Acquiring certificates frequently entails a comprehensive evaluation by impartial third-party entities, hence enhancing the legitimacy of a company's quality assertions.

Contrarily, compliance describes abiding by rules, laws, and industry standards established by governing organizations or trade groups. Financial penalties, legal ramifications, and reputational harm to the business may result from non-compliance. Regulations in several industries mandate that companies gain certain certificates in order to operate lawfully. By demonstrating a company's dedication to quality and adherence to established norms, these certifications serve to foster trust among partners and customers.

A strong framework for quality control and standards must include measures to ensure product quality, fulfill industry standards, and achieve certifications. By guaranteeing regulatory compliance, encouraging a culture of continuous improvement, and cultivating customer happiness, they collectively contribute to the overall profitability and sustainability of enterprises.

MARKETING TACTICS FOR YOUR RADISH FARM'S BRAND

Establishing a unique character in the market for your radish farm requires developing a strong brand. A great brand is more than simply a name or logo; it's an expression of your radishes' character, excellence, and values. Determine your radishes' USPs first, such as their freshness, distinctive types, or environmentally friendly growing methods. Craft a captivating brand narrative that appeals to your intended audience, emphasizing the process from seed to harvest. To strengthen the brand image, branding must be consistent throughout packaging, marketing collateral, and the company's website.

FORMULATING A MARKETING STRATEGY

A clearly defined marketing strategy is your radish farm's road map to success. To start, gather information about consumer preferences, market trends, and rivals by performing market research. Determine who your target market is and adjust your marketing tactics accordingly. To reach a larger audience, combine traditional and digital marketing channels including email advertising, social media, and content marketing. Whether your objective is to increase revenue, increase market share, or raise brand awareness, make sure it is well-defined. To keep ahead of the competition, evaluate and modify your plan on a regular basis in response to feedback and shifting market conditions.

SALES CHANNELS AND DISTRIBUTION

Choosing the appropriate sales channels and distribution strategies is essential to certain that your items are effectively delivered to customers' hands. To vary your sales channels, investigate a range of options, including restaurants, farmers' markets, neighborhood grocery shops, and internet platforms. You can build a devoted following and highlight the variety of your radishes by partnering with nearby businesses or working with chefs.

Make the most of your distribution capabilities to cut down on waste and guarantee that your supply is fresh.

To reach clients who appreciate the convenience of having fresh radishes delivered right to their home, think about introducing direct-to-consumer sales via a website or subscription services. Establishing robust connections with distributors and retailers is crucial for obtaining shelf space and broadening your market penetration. To remain flexible in the face of competition, periodically review and modify your distribution plan in light of customer feedback, seasonal fluctuations, and shifting market dynamics.

CHAPTER SEVEN

MONEY HANDLING

BUDGETING AND EXPENSE CONTROL

Careful planning and resource management are essential components of effective financial management, and budgeting is a key instrument in this process. The methodical process of budgeting entails estimating and assigning financial resources to various organizational operations. It acts as a road map, giving a thorough rundown of projected income and expenses over a given time frame. Budgeting helps firms make educated decisions and match their actions with strategic objectives by defining clear financial goals and constraints.

A key element of budgeting is expense control, which emphasizes cost management and optimization to guarantee long-term financial viability. It entails keeping an eye on and controlling spending to stop unauthorized or needless expenses.

Organizations may pinpoint areas for improvement, put cost-cutting initiatives in place, and increase overall operational efficiency by keeping thorough expense records. Expense control supports the organization's financial stability by preventing financial setbacks and helping to maintain a healthy bottom line.

STRATEGIES FOR PRICING

A business's ability to make money is largely dependent on its pricing methods. A number of aspects need to be carefully considered when determining the appropriate pricing for goods or services, such as perceived value, market demand, competition, and manufacturing costs. A clearly defined pricing strategy complements the organization's positioning in the market and overall company goals.

There are various pricing techniques, including value-based pricing, penetration pricing, cost-plus pricing, and skimming pricing. With cost-plus pricing, prices are set by marking up manufacturing costs in order to pay all expenses and provide a profit margin. Value-based pricing, on the other hand, enables companies to realize the value they offer by focusing on the perceived worth of the good or service to consumers.

While skimming pricing entails setting high prices at first and progressively dropping them, penetration pricing tries to capture market share by setting starting prices lower than competitors. Long-term corporate objectives, product differentiation, and market conditions all influence the price approach that is chosen. Whichever strategy is used, reaching financial goals and maintaining market competitiveness depend on a well-thought-out pricing plan.

ANALYSIS OF PROFITABILITY

A crucial component of financial management is profitability analysis, which measures a company's capacity to turn a profit in order to analyze its overall financial performance. To assess the efficacy and efficiency of an organization's operations, a range of financial parameters, including net profit margin, gross profit margin, and return on investment (ROI), are analyzed.

The gross profit margin can be computed as a percentage of revenue by deducting the cost of products sold from the total revenue. By taking into account all operating costs, taxes, and interest, net profit margin, on the other hand, offers a more complete picture of overall profitability. Businesses can evaluate the efficacy of their investments by using ROI, which measures the return on capital invested.

Profitability analysis explores the variables impacting profit generation in addition to tracking income and expenses. Comprehending the factors that influence profitability enables firms to make well-informed decisions, strategically manage resources, and recognize possibilities for expansion.

CHAPTER EIGHT

ECOLOGICAL METHODS
TECHNIQUES FOR ORGANIC FARMING

Organic farming is a kind of farming that puts an emphasis on sustainability by using only natural processes instead of artificial inputs like fertilizers and pesticides. This approach is based on managing pests and improving soil fertility through the use of biological control and organic materials.

Crop rotation is a fundamental tenet of organic farming since it helps preserve soil health and lowers the likelihood of pest infestations. Furthermore, organic farmers place a strong emphasis on biodiversity, using polyculture and companion planting to produce a balanced ecosystem that encourages resilience in the face of environmental challenges and supports natural pest control.

ENVIRONMENTAL IMPACT

The environmental impact of sustainability measures, especially in agriculture, needs to be taken into account. Because organic farming practices use less chemicals, which can contaminate water and soil, they have a favorable environmental impact. Organic farming helps preserve ecosystem health and biodiversity by avoiding synthetic fertilizers and pesticides. Additionally, the use of green manure and cover crops, which improve soil fertility and lower the danger of soil erosion, is common in organic farming. Organic farming prioritizes these techniques, which reduces adverse environmental externalities and promotes a more harmonious relationship between agriculture and the natural world.

SOCIAL RESPONSIBILITY

Sustainability techniques in agriculture encompass social responsibility as well as environmental considerations.

Fair labor practices and local community support are generally given priority in organic farming operations. Employment opportunities can arise from the usage of organic farming, especially in small-scale farming operations. Furthermore, the focus on community-based agriculture strengthens the bonds between farmers and customers and promotes a feeling of shared accountability for the environment and human well-being. In sustainable agriculture, social responsibility also entails encouraging fair distribution of resources and giving underprivileged groups the tools they need to engage in organic farming and reap its benefits. In this sense, sustainability is a commitment to promoting social justice and the well-being of communities as well as an environmental necessity.

CHAPTER NINE

PROBLEMS AND SOLUTIONS

TYPICAL OBSTACLES IN RADISH PRODUCTION

Like any agricultural enterprise, raising radishes is not without its difficulties. Radish producers frequently encounter the issue of radishes being vulnerable to different pests and illnesses. Aphids, flea beetles, and root maggots are just a few of the pests that can seriously harm radish crops, resulting in lower yields and deteriorated quality. Furthermore, radish plants arc susceptible to diseases like powdery mildew, black rot, and damping-off. Integrated pest management (IPM) techniques can be used to solve these issues. This strategy reduces the negative effects of pests and diseases on radish crops by combining biological, cultural, and chemical control techniques.

The effect of environmental elements on crop growth, such as temperature and soil conditions, is another difficulty in radish cultivation.

Cool weather is ideal for radishes, while high or low temperatures might cause poor germination and stunted development. When growing radish, soil quality and moisture content are also very important factors. These difficulties can be lessened by choosing cultivars that are appropriate for a given environment and putting good irrigation techniques into practice. Furthermore, mulching can help maintain uniform soil temperature and moisture, which promotes ideal radish development.

Another obstacle for radish growers is the ever-evolving market and shifting consumer tastes. Seasonality and food trends are two variables that can affect the demand for radishes. To overcome this difficulty, growers should broaden the range of radish types they offer, satisfying the varying tastes of the market and increasing radishes' year-round availability. A more steady and dependable market for radish vegetables can also be created by forming alliances with nearby markets, grocers, and eateries.

METHODS OF SOLVING PROBLEMS

A common problem for farmers is the cost and availability of inputs, such as herbicides, fertilizers, and seeds. Success in radish farming depends on having access to inexpensive inputs and high-quality seeds. Farmers can overcome these obstacles through cooperative farming arrangements and partnerships with agricultural extension agencies, which facilitate group purchasing, information exchange, and bulk discounts on inputs.

Labor-intensive and time-consuming processes in the cultivation of radish can be caused by inefficient agricultural practices and a lack of mechanization. Farmers can use contemporary, mechanized agricultural methods, such precision planting and harvesting equipment, to overcome this difficulty.

In radish farming, mechanization not only lowers labor costs but also increases production and efficiency.

Managing pests and diseases, environmental conditions, market dynamics, input availability, and farming practices are only a few of the difficulties faced by radish farmers. To overcome these obstacles and guarantee a more successful and sustainable radish farming endeavor, problem-solving techniques including integrated pest control, appropriate crop selection, diversity, cooperative farming, and mechanization can be put into practice.